Additional Colle

Church House Publishing

Published by Church House Publishing
Church House
Great Smith Street
London SW1P 3NZ

Telephone 020 7898 1451
Fax 020 7898 1449

Copyright © *The Archbishops' Council 2004*

ISBN 0 7151 2087 5

All rights reserved — No part of this publication may be reproduced in any form or by any means, electronic or mechanical, including photocopying, recording or any information storage and retrieval system, except as stated below, without written permission.

Texts for local use — The arrangements which apply to local editions of services cover reproduction on a non-commercial basis both for a single occasion and for repeated use. Details are available in the booklet *A Brief Guide to Liturgical Copyright* (see Copyright Information on page 29 for further information).

Printed and bound by ArklePrint Ltd, Northampton
on 80 gsm Dutchman Ivory

Designed and typeset by John Morgan studio

Contents

Introduction

The Additional Collects were commissioned in response to a request for 'additional collects in a worthy contemporary idiom'. They are intended to be

¶ short,
¶ simple in their syntax,
¶ vivid and interesting in their themes and imagery,
¶ accessible in the kind of language they use,

and to say something which is clear and distinct. All of them are based on new composition.

The Additional Collects incorporate petitions, ideas and metaphors drawn from reflection upon Scripture, upon the season of the Church's year (except in Ordinary Time), upon key theological themes, and upon the general experience of being a Christian today (but also in the light of the history of Christian faith and discipleship down the centuries).

As with most collects, these prayers are usually addressed to the Father and end with a pleading through Christ. Some, however, are addressed directly to the Son. These are for festivals marking events in the life of Christ: Christmas Day, the Presentation of Christ in the Temple, Palm Sunday, Ascension Day and the Sundays of Easter except Easter Day and Pentecost. The Collect for Pentecost is unique in being addressed to the Spirit. The Collects for the Sundays of Easter which are addressed to the Son have a common ending: 'to the glory of God the Father' (in the case of the Second Sunday of Easter, 'to the praise of God the Father').

The seasons make their mark on the Collects, with each one in a season reflecting something of the season's themes and flavour. The Advent Collects are not quite so strongly thematic as the original *Common Worship* Collects, but those for the Third and Fourth Sundays relate to the work of John the Baptist and the Blessed Virgin Mary respectively. The Epiphany Collects tend to make reference to the missionary work of the Gospel. The Lenten Collects, unsurprisingly, contain the themes of self-discipline and struggle against sin and evil, becoming more focused on the Cross from the Fifth Sunday of Lent onwards. The Easter Collects contain recollections of gospel accounts of the disciples' encounters with the risen Christ. The Collects for Ascension Day, Trinity Sunday and Christ the King all contain explicit reference to the immanent life of the Holy Trinity.

For Sundays, the Principal Feasts which may fall on Sundays, and Principal Holy Days, *Common Worship* now provides two sets of collects. The original *Common Worship* Collects stand firmly in the classical collect tradition, drawing heavily on *The Book of Common Prayer* and more recent Anglican sources, but also including new compositions. The Additional Collects seek to develop that tradition further: these are simple and short prayers which are recognizably in the Anglican tradition of collect-writing, whilst having an accessible and contemporary style of language. The two sets of collects are intended to complement each other. It is envisaged that on each occasion those conducting services will choose the collect which they consider more suitable for the particular service and congregation.

Notes

1 Normally on any occasion only one Collect is used.

2 The Collect for each Sunday is used on the following weekdays, except where other provision is made.

3 At Evening Prayer on Saturdays other than Easter Eve, Christmas Eve or Principal Feasts or Festivals, the Collect appointed for the ensuing Sunday shall be used. When Evening Prayer on the day before a Festival makes use of the lessons relating to that Festival, the Collect of that Festival shall be used.

4 A number of Collects are designated **. In each season, the designated Collect may replace the Collect of the Day on other Sundays in that season. In Ordinary Time (the Sundays before Lent, the Sundays after Trinity and the Sundays before Advent) one of the designated Collects for Ordinary Time may replace the Collect of the Day.

¶ *Advent*

The First Sunday of Advent *Purple*

Almighty God,
as your kingdom dawns,
turn us from the darkness of sin to the
    light of holiness,
that we may be ready to meet you
in our Lord and Saviour, Jesus Christ.

The Second Sunday of Advent *Purple*

Almighty God,
purify our hearts and minds,
that when your Son Jesus Christ comes again as
    judge and saviour
we may be ready to receive him,
who is our Lord and our God.

The Third Sunday of Advent *Purple*

God for whom we watch and wait,
you sent John the Baptist to prepare the way of your Son:
give us courage to speak the truth,
to hunger for justice,
and to suffer for the cause of right,
with Jesus Christ our Lord.

The Fourth Sunday of Advent ** *Purple*

This provision is not used on weekdays after 23 December.

Eternal God,
as Mary waited for the birth of your Son,
so we wait for his coming in glory;
bring us through the birth pangs of this present age
to see, with her, our great salvation
in Jesus Christ our Lord.

24 December

Christmas Eve *Purple*

Almighty God,
as we prepare with joy
to celebrate the gift of the Christ-child,
embrace the earth with your glory
and be for us a living hope
in Jesus Christ our Lord.

¶ Christmas

Christmas Night

25 December *Principal Feast* *Gold or White*

Eternal God,
in the stillness of this night
you sent your almighty Word
to pierce the world's darkness with the light of salvation:
give to the earth the peace that we long for
and fill our hearts with the joy of heaven
through our Saviour, Jesus Christ.

Christmas Day **

25 December *Principal Feast* *Gold or White*

Lord Jesus Christ,
your birth at Bethlehem
draws us to kneel in wonder at heaven touching earth:
accept our heartfelt praise
as we worship you,
our Saviour and our eternal God.

The First Sunday of Christmas *White*

This provision is not used on weekdays after 5 January.

God in Trinity,
eternal unity of perfect love:
gather the nations to be one family,
and draw us into your holy life
through the birth of Emmanuel,
our Lord Jesus Christ.

The Second Sunday of Christmas *White*

This provision is not used on weekdays after 5 January.

God our Father,
in love you sent your Son
that the world may have life:
lead us to seek him among the outcast
and to find him in those in need,
for Jesus Christ's sake.

¶ *Epiphany*

The Epiphany

6 January

Principal Feast

Gold or White

Creator of the heavens,
who led the Magi by a star
to worship the Christ-child:
guide and sustain us,
that we may find our journey's end
in Jesus Christ our Lord.

The Baptism of Christ

The First Sunday of Epiphany

Gold or White

Heavenly Father,
at the Jordan you revealed Jesus as your Son:
may we recognize him as our Lord
and know ourselves to be your beloved children;
through Jesus Christ our Saviour.

The Second Sunday of Epiphany **

White

Eternal Lord,
our beginning and our end:
bring us with the whole creation
to your glory, hidden through past ages
and made known
in Jesus Christ our Lord.

The Third Sunday of Epiphany

White

God of all mercy,
your Son proclaimed good news to the poor,
release to the captives,
and freedom to the oppressed:
anoint us with your Holy Spirit
and set all your people free
to praise you in Christ our Lord.

The Fourth Sunday of Epiphany

White

God of heaven,
you send the gospel to the ends of the earth
and your messengers to every nation:
send your Holy Spirit to transform us
by the good news of everlasting life
in Jesus Christ our Lord.

2 February

The Presentation of Christ in the Temple

Gold or White

Candlemas

Principal Feast

Lord Jesus Christ,
light of the nations and glory of Israel:
make your home among us,
and present us pure and holy
to your heavenly Father,
your God, and our God.

The Fifth Sunday before Lent

Green

This provision is always used from the day after the Presentation of Christ in the Temple until the first of the Sundays before Lent.

God of our salvation,
help us to turn away from those habits which harm our bodies
and poison our minds
and to choose again your gift of life,
revealed to us in Jesus Christ our Lord.

The Fourth Sunday before Lent

Green

Lord of the hosts of heaven,
our salvation and our strength,
without you we are lost:
guard us from all that harms or hurts
and raise us when we fall;
through Jesus Christ our Lord.

The Third Sunday before Lent

Green

Eternal God,
whose Son went among the crowds
and brought healing with his touch:
help us to show his love,
in your Church as we gather together,
and by our lives as they are transformed
into the image of Christ our Lord.

The Second Sunday before Lent ** *Green*

Almighty God,
give us reverence for all creation
and respect for every person,
that we may mirror your likeness
in Jesus Christ our Lord.

The Sunday next before Lent *Green*

This provision is not used on or after Ash Wednesday.

Holy God,
you know the disorder of our sinful lives:
set straight our crooked hearts,
and bend our wills to love your goodness
  and your glory
in Jesus Christ our Lord.

Ash Wednesday

Principal Holy Day

Purple or Lent Array

Holy God,
our lives are laid open before you:
rescue us from the chaos of sin
and through the death of your Son
bring us healing and make us whole
in Jesus Christ our Lord.

The First Sunday of Lent

Purple or Lent Array

Heavenly Father,
your Son battled with the powers of darkness,
and grew closer to you in the desert:
help us to use these days to grow in wisdom and prayer
that we may witness to your saving love
in Jesus Christ our Lord.

The Second Sunday of Lent **

Purple or Lent Array

Almighty God,
by the prayer and discipline of Lent
may we enter into the mystery of Christ's sufferings,
and by following in his Way
come to share in his glory;
through Jesus Christ our Lord.

The Third Sunday of Lent

Purple or Lent Array

Eternal God,
give us insight
to discern your will for us,
to give up what harms us,
and to seek the perfection we are promised
in Jesus Christ our Lord.

The Fourth Sunday of Lent

Purple or Lent Array

Mothering Sunday may be celebrated in preference to the provision for the Fourth Sunday of Lent.

Merciful Lord,
you know our struggle to serve you:
when sin spoils our lives
and overshadows our hearts,
come to our aid
and turn us back to you again;
through Jesus Christ our Lord.

Mothering Sunday

Purple or Lent Array

God of love,
passionate and strong,
tender and careful:
watch over us and hold us
all the days of our life;
through Jesus Christ our Lord.

The Fifth Sunday of Lent

Passiontide begins

Purple or Lent Array

Gracious Father,
you gave up your Son
out of love for the world:
lead us to ponder the mysteries of his passion,
that we may know eternal peace
through the shedding of our Saviour's blood,
Jesus Christ our Lord.

Palm Sunday *Red*

True and humble king,
hailed by the crowd as Messiah:
grant us the faith to know you and love you,
that we may be found beside you
on the way of the cross,
which is the path of glory.

Maundy Thursday *White*

Principal Holy Day

At Morning and Evening Prayer the Collect of Palm Sunday is used.
At Holy Communion this Collect is used.

God our Father,
your Son Jesus Christ was obedient to the end
and drank the cup prepared for him:
may we who share his table
watch with him through the night of suffering
and be faithful.

Good Friday

Principal Holy Day

Hangings removed: red for the liturgy

Eternal God,
in the cross of Jesus
we see the cost of our sin
and the depth of your love:
in humble hope and fear
may we place at his feet
all that we have and all that we are,
through Jesus Christ our Lord.

Easter Eve

Hangings removed

In the depths of our isolation
we cry to you, Lord God:
give light in our darkness
and bring us out of the prison of our despair;
through Jesus Christ our Lord.

¶ *Easter*

Easter Day *Gold or White*

Principal Feast

God of glory,
by the raising of your Son
you have broken the chains of death and hell:
fill your Church with faith and hope;
for a new day has dawned
and the way to life stands open
in our Saviour Jesus Christ.

The Second Sunday of Easter *White*

Risen Christ,
for whom no door is locked, no entrance barred:
open the doors of our hearts,
that we may seek the good of others
and walk the joyful road of sacrifice and peace,
to the praise of God the Father.

The Third Sunday of Easter ** *White*

Risen Christ,
you filled your disciples with boldness and fresh hope:
strengthen us to proclaim your risen life
and fill us with your peace,
to the glory of God the Father.

The Fourth Sunday of Easter *White*

Risen Christ,
faithful shepherd of your Father's sheep:
teach us to hear your voice
and to follow your command,
that all your people may be gathered into one flock,
to the glory of God the Father.

The Fifth Sunday of Easter *White*

Risen Christ,
your wounds declare your love for the world
and the wonder of your risen life:
give us compassion and courage
to risk ourselves for those we serve,
to the glory of God the Father.

The Sixth Sunday of Easter *White*

This provision is not used on or after Ascension Day.

Risen Christ,
by the lakeside you renewed your call to your disciples:
help your Church to obey your command
and draw the nations to the fire of your love,
to the glory of God the Father.

Ascension Day

Principal Feast

Gold or White

Risen Christ,
you have raised our human nature to the throne of heaven:
help us to seek and serve you,
that we may join you at the Father's side,
where you reign with the Spirit in glory,
now and for ever.

The Seventh Sunday of Easter

Sunday after Ascension Day

White

Risen, ascended Lord,
as we rejoice at your triumph,
fill your Church on earth with power and compassion,
that all who are estranged by sin
may find forgiveness and know your peace,
to the glory of God the Father.

Day of Pentecost

Whit Sunday

Principal Feast

Red

This provision is not used on the weekdays after the Day of Pentecost.

Holy Spirit, sent by the Father,
ignite in us your holy fire;
strengthen your children with the gift of faith,
revive your Church with the breath of love,
and renew the face of the earth,
through Jesus Christ our Lord.

Trinity Sunday

Principal Feast

Gold or White

Holy God,
faithful and unchanging:
enlarge our minds with the knowledge of your truth,
and draw us more deeply into the mystery of your love,
that we may truly worship you,
Father, Son and Holy Spirit,
one God, now and for ever.

The First Sunday after Trinity

Green

God of truth,
help us to keep your law of love
and to walk in ways of wisdom,
that we may find true life
in Jesus Christ your Son.

The Second Sunday after Trinity

Green

Faithful Creator,
whose mercy never fails:
deepen our faithfulness to you
and to your living Word,
Jesus Christ our Lord.

The Third Sunday after Trinity **

Green

God our saviour,
look on this wounded world
in pity and in power;
hold us fast to your promises of peace
won for us by your Son,
our Saviour Jesus Christ.

The Fourth Sunday after Trinity *Green*

Gracious Father,
by the obedience of Jesus
you brought salvation to our wayward world:
draw us into harmony with your will,
that we may find all things restored in him,
our Saviour Jesus Christ.

The Fifth Sunday after Trinity *Green*

Almighty God,
send down upon your Church
the riches of your Spirit,
and kindle in all who minister the gospel
your countless gifts of grace;
through Jesus Christ our Lord.

The Sixth Sunday after Trinity *Green*

Creator God,
you made us all in your image:
may we discern you in all that we see,
and serve you in all that we do;
through Jesus Christ our Lord.

The Seventh Sunday after Trinity *Green*

Generous God,
you give us gifts and make them grow:
though our faith is small as mustard seed,
make it grow to your glory
and the flourishing of your kingdom;
through Jesus Christ our Lord.

The Eighth Sunday after Trinity ** *Green*

Lord God,
your Son left the riches of heaven
and became poor for our sake:
when we prosper save us from pride,
when we are needy save us from despair,
that we may trust in you alone;
through Jesus Christ our Lord.

The Ninth Sunday after Trinity *Green*

Gracious Father,
revive your Church in our day,
and make her holy, strong and faithful,
for your glory's sake
in Jesus Christ our Lord.

The Tenth Sunday after Trinity *Green*

Lord of heaven and earth,
as Jesus taught his disciples to be persistent in prayer,
give us patience and courage never to lose hope,
but always to bring our prayers before you;
through Jesus Christ our Lord.

The Eleventh Sunday after Trinity *Green*

God of glory,
the end of our searching,
help us to lay aside
all that prevents us from seeking your kingdom,
and to give all that we have
to gain the pearl beyond all price,
through our Saviour Jesus Christ.

The Twelfth Sunday after Trinity ** *Green*

God of constant mercy,
who sent your Son to save us:
remind us of your goodness,
increase your grace within us,
that our thankfulness may grow,
through Jesus Christ our Lord.

The Thirteenth Sunday after Trinity *Green*

Almighty God,
you search us and know us:
may we rely on you in strength
and rest on you in weakness,
now and in all our days;
through Jesus Christ our Lord.

The Fourteenth Sunday after Trinity *Green*

Merciful God,
your Son came to save us
and bore our sins on the cross:
may we trust in your mercy
and know your love,
rejoicing in the righteousness
that is ours through Jesus Christ our Lord.

The Fifteenth Sunday after Trinity *Green*

Lord God,
defend your Church from all false teaching
and give to your people knowledge of your truth,
that we may enjoy eternal life
in Jesus Christ our Lord.

The Sixteenth Sunday after Trinity *Green*

Lord of creation,
whose glory is around and within us:
open our eyes to your wonders,
that we may serve you with reverence
and know your peace at our lives' end,
through Jesus Christ our Lord.

The Seventeenth Sunday after Trinity *Green*

Gracious God,
you call us to fullness of life:
deliver us from unbelief
and banish our anxieties
with the liberating love of Jesus Christ our Lord.

The Eighteenth Sunday after Trinity *Green*

God, our judge and saviour,
teach us to be open to your truth
and to trust in your love,
that we may live each day
with confidence in the salvation which is given
through Jesus Christ our Lord.

The Nineteenth Sunday after Trinity *Green*

Faithful Lord,
whose steadfast love never ceases
and whose mercies never come to an end:
grant us the grace to trust you
and to receive the gifts of your love,
new every morning,
in Jesus Christ our Lord.

The Twentieth Sunday after Trinity *Green*

God, our light and our salvation:
illuminate our lives,
that we may see your goodness in the land of the living,
and looking on your beauty
may be changed into the likeness of Jesus Christ our Lord.

The Twenty-first Sunday after Trinity *Green*

Almighty God,
in whose service lies perfect freedom:
teach us to obey you
with loving hearts and steadfast wills;
through Jesus Christ our Lord.

If there are twenty-three Sundays after Trinity, the provision for the Third Sunday before Lent (page 10) is used on the Twenty-second Sunday after Trinity.

The Last Sunday after Trinity *Green*

Merciful God,
teach us to be faithful in change and uncertainty,
that trusting in your word
and obeying your will
we may enter the unfailing joy of Jesus Christ our Lord.

1 November **All Saints' Day** *Gold or White*

Principal Feast

God of holiness,
your glory is proclaimed in every age:
as we rejoice in the faith of your saints,
inspire us to follow their example
with boldness and joy;
through Jesus Christ our Lord.

The Fourth Sunday before Advent

Red or Green

God of glory,
touch our lips with the fire of your Spirit,
that we with all creation
may rejoice to sing your praise;
through Jesus Christ our Lord.

The Third Sunday before Advent **

Red or Green

God, our refuge and strength,
bring near the day when wars shall cease
and poverty and pain shall end,
that earth may know the peace of heaven
through Jesus Christ our Lord.

In years when Remembrance Sunday is observed on the Second Sunday before Advent, the Collect and Post Communion for the Third Sunday before Advent may be used on Remembrance Sunday and the Collect and Post Communion for the Second Sunday before Advent may be used on the Third Sunday before Advent.

The Second Sunday before Advent

Red or Green

Heavenly Lord,
you long for the world's salvation:
stir us from apathy,
restrain us from excess
and revive in us new hope
that all creation will one day be healed
in Jesus Christ our Lord.

Christ the King

The Sunday next before Advent

Red or White

God the Father,
help us to hear the call of Christ the King
and to follow in his service,
whose kingdom has no end;
for he reigns with you and the Holy Spirit,
one God, one glory.

Harvest Thanksgiving *Green*

Harvest Thanksgiving may be celebrated on a Sunday and may replace the provision for that day, provided it does not supersede any Principal Feast or Festival.

Creator God,
you made the goodness of the land,
the riches of the sea
and the rhythm of the seasons;
as we thank you for the harvest,
may we cherish and respect
this planet and its peoples,
through Jesus Christ our Lord.

Authorization

¶ The Collects in this publication are authorized pursuant to Canon B 2 of the Canons of the Church of England for use until further resolution of the General Synod.

Copyright Information

The Archbishops' Council of the Church of England and the other copyright owners and administrators of texts included in *Common Worship: Services and Prayers for the Church of England* have given permission for the use of their material in local reproductions on a non-commercial basis which comply with the conditions for reproductions for local use set out in the Archbishops' Council's booklet, *A Brief Guide to Liturgical Copyright*. This is available from

Church House Bookshop
Great Smith Street
London SW1P 3BN
Telephone: 020 7898 1300/1/2/4/6
Fax: 020 7898 1305
Email: bookshop@c-of-e.org.uk

or from www.cofe.anglican.org/commonworship. A reproduction which meets the conditions stated in that booklet may be made without an application for copyright permission or payment of a fee, but the following copyright acknowledgement must be included:

> *Common Worship: Services and Prayers for the Church of England*, material from which is included in this service, is copyright © The Archbishops' Council 2000.

Permission must be obtained in advance for any reproduction which does not comply with the conditions set out in *A Brief Guide to Liturgical Copyright*. Applications for permission should be addressed to:

The Copyright Administrator
The Archbishops' Council
Church House
Great Smith Street
London SW1P 3NZ
Telephone: 020 7898 1451
Fax: 020 7898 1449
Email: copyright@c-of-e.org.uk

Related Publications

Common Worship: Collects and Post Communions

This publication contains all of the *Common Worship* Collects and Post Communions in Contemporary Language, including the Additional Collects.

Collects and Post Communions in Traditional Language for Lesser Festivals, Common of the Saints and Special Occasions

This publication contains those *Common Worship* Collects and Post Communions in Traditional Language which are not included in the main volume (*Common Worship: Services and Prayers for the Church of England*).